Greetings from
Savannah

4880 Lower Valley Road, Atglen, PA 19310 USA

Mary L. Martin, Tina Skinner,
Nathaniel Wolfgang-Price, and
Preface by John Duncan

Preface

Collecting postcards is a hobby that can begin early and last a lifetime. As a twelfth generation Charlestonian I collected Charleston postcards for twenty years and in 1965 when I came to Savannah to teach history at Armstrong Junior College I began collecting Savannah postcards. At last count my Savannah postcard collection numbered over 4,000. My wife calls it an obsession but this is a collecting obsession that does not take up lots of space. Moreover prices, at least for the beginning collector, are not prohibitive. I remember the local flea market offering Savannah postcards for one cent each in the late 1970s.

Obviously, some cards can be expensive. I once paid $75.00 for a c. 1920 photo postcard of two local African-American children dressed as Indian braves. And every collector has a story of the one that got away. In my case it was a card offered on eBay showing ladies in long dresses and floppy hats opening oysters at Tybee circa 1910. My, how I wish I had gotten that one.

It's a wide spectrum of people who buy and collect postcards. Savannahians like to collect local postcards and the thousands of tourists who visit our city buy Savannah cards and send them all over the world. For ten years our shop V. & J. Duncan Antique Maps, Prints & Books gave postcards of our shop dog Rosie to our customers and we like to think that her image has graced refrigerators in every state and a few foreign countries. Midnight author John Berendt has collected Savannah postcards for 25 years and one can only wonder if the publication of his "The City of Falling Angels" has led him to a Venice collection.

Postcards may not be in the same category as fine paintings and sculpture but they can be quite beautiful in their own right and are a rich source of history. They show us where we are and where we have been and as such are a gold mine of images present and past.

John Duncan
November 2005
Savannah, Georgia

Published by Schiffer Publishing Ltd.
4880 Lower Valley Road
Atglen, PA 19310
Phone: (610) 593-1777; Fax: (610) 593-2002
E-mail: Info@schifferbooks.com

For the largest selection of fine reference books on this and related subjects, please visit our web site at
www.schifferbooks.com
We are always looking for people to write books on new and related subjects. If you have an idea for a book please contact us at the above address.

This book may be purchased from the publisher.
Include $3.95 for shipping.
Please try your bookstore first.
You may write for a free catalog.

In Europe, Schiffer books are distributed by
Bushwood Books
6 Marksbury Ave.
Kew Gardens
Surrey TW9 4JF England
Phone: 44 (0) 20 8392-8585; Fax: 44 (0) 20 8392-9876
E-mail: info@bushwoodbooks.co.uk
Website: www.bushwoodbooks.co.uk
Free postage in the U.K., Europe; air mail at cost.

Contents

Introduction 4

History

In the Beginning 5
The Revolutionary War 7
The Civil War 13
Fort Screven 16
Plantation Life 22

The City

Squares and Monuments 27
Scenery 29
Streets 42

Government Buildings and Schools 57
Churches 68
Banks 77
Houses and Buildings of Note 82
Industry 88

Tourism

Sports 104
Hotels 110
Islands and Beaches 122

Bibliography 128

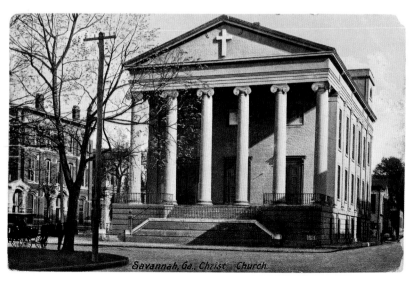

Savannah, Ga. Christ Church.

Introduction

Savannah is, above all else, a beautiful city. Tourists have journeyed here for over a century to walk among its splendid concentration of architecturally impressive mansions, punctuated by stately oaks draped in curtains of Spanish moss and the monuments and fountains that are sprinkled throughout the city's series of small parks called squares although most are indeed rectangles.

Savannah had its beginnings as a plan of James Edward Oglethorpe who, along with settlers, came aboard the galley *Anne* to the area that would become Savannah on February 12, 1733. Oglethorpe's plan called for the construction of four wards. Each with forty building lots; four trust lots, and one square in the middle. Each building lot was given space for one five-acre garden just outside town and almost forty-five acres of farmland further south. The trust lots were set aside for public buildings like courthouses and churches, and the squares were common ground to be used by all the ward's residents.

Eventually Savannah's location as Atlantic port conduit for the fertile plantation lands inland made the city and a number of its residents very wealthy during a boom in the cotton trade. The same accessibility that made Savannah so prosperous also made the city a destination for tourists. Like a proper Southern Lady, Savannah was more than prepared to welcome these callers.

Known as the "Hostess City" Savannah is home to a year-round tourist industry that attracts millions of visitors. Visitors come from every part of the globe to tour Savannah's two-and-a-half mile long Historic District, packed with elegant Greek revival and Victorian mansions as well as the beautiful squares and sprawling parks.

With so many beauty spots in Savannah and so many tourists arriving annually it seemed only natural that the postcard industry would take advantage of the situation and soon postcards from Savannah were being sent to the far corners of the world by captivated tourists wishing to share the beauty they found in Savannah with friends and family. In this book, postcards from the turn of the century through the mid 1950s help illustrate Savannah as she once was. Because of the remarkable efforts of preservationists, much of what is shown in the book still stands today, and these valuable images helps serve as a record for her future preservation.

History

The Beginning

Sent out by King George II of England with a charter to establish the Colony of Georgia in America, James Edward Oglethorpe and the first Georgia colonists arrived in the New World in February 1733. Oglethorpe proclaimed the new colony and Savannah became its first town.

The new colony of Georgia would strengthen the colonies by increasing trade. Georgia could also act as a buffer zone for South Carolina, protecting it from the advance of the Spaniards in Florida. Under the original charter, all individuals, except papists were free to worship as they pleased. Rum, lawyers, and slavery were forbidden for a time. A brewing battle between local Indian tribes and the new settlers was averted by Chief Tomochichi of the Yamacraw people. He negotiated peace and pledged his friendship with Oglethorpe. The new arrivals were granted permission to settle Savannah on the bluff, and the colony enjoyed peace with the natives, a rare luxury in the New World. One tribe member married settler John Musgrove. Mary Musgrove, as she came to be known, acted as an interpreter for the colonists and ran a trading post that offered a useful service to both groups. Thus Savannah enjoyed a peaceful beginning.

Oglethorpe is credited with establishing America's best planned town. He laid a series of grids that allowed for wide-open streets intertwined with public squares that served as town meeting places and centers of business. The city would eventually have twenty-four original squares, twenty-two of which are still in existence.

BURIAL PLACE OF INDIAN CHIEF TOMO-CHI-CHI, FRIEND OF GEN. OGLETHORPE, SAVANNAH, GA.—51

The monument to Indian Chief Tomochichi, who welcomed Oglethorpe and the first Georgian settlers. After facilitating peace between the settlers and the Creek Indian tribes, Tomochichi traveled to England to meet the king and queen. When Tomochichi died in 1739, Oglethorpe buried him in Percival, now Wright Square. On the sixtieth anniversary of his death, the Colonial Dames had a huge rock from Stone Mountain brought to the site to honor his memory.

Circa 1930; $2-4

OGLETHORPE MONUMENT, SAVANNAH, GA.—50

Daniel Chester French's Oglethorpe Monument in Chippewa Square was finished in 1910. The corners display the coat of arms for the Oglethorpe family and the seal of the State of Georgia. The pedestal was created by New York architect Henry Bacon.

Circa 1920; $3-5

Revolutionary War

Georgia was the least populated of the thirteen American colonies in the 1770s. Half its inhabitants were slaves, and most were clustered near the coast. As the northern colonies fumed under the imposition of new tax laws from England, Georgians continued apace, expressing some concerns that the molasses tax and new shipping regulations imposed by the crown might harm trade in lumber with Caribbean colonies. They weren't overly concerned, though, and the Georgia leaders simply authorized South Carolina to represent them at the first Continental Congress in 1774. At the second congress, the other colonies acted upon concerns regarding Georgia's loyalist tendencies and elected to cut off trade with the youngest colony.

However, at the same time a band of patriots in Lexington, Massachusetts fired at British troops, and rebels began mobilizing throughout the colonies. In June, 1775, Georgia patriots began stockpiling munitions, and sending aid to besieged patriots in Boston.

Royal Governor Sir James Wright wrote a letter requesting additional troops and boats to protect his colony's loyalists, but the letter was intercepted by the South Carolina Committee of Correspondence, and new documents were forged stating that all was well within the Georgia colony.

However, the war was slow to come so far south. In 1778, London sent out orders targeting the South as the main theater of war. British warships were rerouted from New York Harbor toward South Carolina and Georgia. Savannah fell with little resistance to Major General Prevost, and the small community was quickly converted back to British control. Royal Governor Sir James Wright returned in July of 1779, charged with rolling back the clocks to the way things stood two years earlier when he was in power.

In an attempt to regain the city, Major General Benjamin Lincoln, southern commander of the Continental Army, and French Admiral Valerie D'Estaing plotted a siege of the city, and Georgia rebels continued to plot in exile. George Washington, now painfully aware of the danger of losing in the South, dispatched General Casimir Pulaski and his "Polish Legion" or cavalry.

Savannah's coastal location, naturally reinforced by creeks and marshes, made it easy to defend. D'Estaing arrived on September 1, 1779, and instead of pursuing what may have been an easy capture of the lightly reinforced city, he waited for the Continental Army to arrive. In the meantime, General Provost was able to reinforce the city's defenses. Eight days later, when the Continental Army began to take up positions around the city, which continued to reinforce its defenses. By October 4th there was still no sign of a British surrender, so Admiral D'Estaing moved his ships into position and began a naval bombardment of the city. The British continued improvements to the city's defenses. Finally Lincoln and D'Estaing agreed to attack the British positions across a broad front on October 9th. The Americans made some progress before the British Regulars under the command of Col. John Maitland, turned back the combined French and Continental Army. Sgt. William Jasper, trying to rally his men to hold the line against the British, grabbed the colors from the wall of the Spring Hill redoubt, but was mortally wounded by British fire. As the American line continued to crumble, General Pulaski rode up and tried to rally the men, and he too was mortally wounded. Pulaski and Jasper were carried back by retreating Americans, but the colors remained in British hands.

5580 Gordon's Monument, Savannah, Ga.

Gordon Monument, Wright Square. Originally named for Viscount Percival, who headed the trustees backing the founding of Georgia, the square was renamed in 1763 in honor of Royal Governor Sir James Wright, who came to Savannah in 1760 and enjoyed several years of popularity. Born in America, the governor ran into trouble when he was charged with enforcing the crown's controversial tax policies. Georgia patriots, the Liberty Boys, advocated immediate independence from England and the imprisonment of Wright, but he escaped and fled to England. He returned after the British took Savannah by force in 1779, but was forced to leave once again when the Americans returned at the end of the war. Wright is now interred at Westminster Abbey.

Circa 1900; $3-5

Wright Square has maintained its name, though the statuary within does not pay honor to the British leader. This card shows the base of the Gordon Monument, a tribute to William Washington Gordon, founder of the Central of Georgia Railroad Banking Company.

Circa 1930-40; $2-4

Jasper Monument, Savannah, Ga

A monument to William Jasper, a military sergeant who died after trying to save his South Carolina flag from the British during the Second Battle of Savannah, was dedicated in Madison Square in 1888.

Cancelled 1922; $5-8

Circa 1910; $5-8

Later postcards show the city growing up around the statue of Jasper, a Revolutionary War hero.

JASPER MONUMENT AND MASONIC TEMPLE, SAVANNAH, GA.

Circa 1930; $4-6

Cancelled 1908; $5-8

9

Count Pulaski's Monument Savannah, Ga.

From the back: "Pulaski Monument, erected in honor of the great general who, with LaFayette, helped George Washington drive the English from our shores and establish freedom and independence."

Cancelled 1918; $5-8

The Pulaski Monument in Monterey Square.

Cancelled 1909; $5-8

Another survivor of the 1779 battle was Lachlan McIntosh. Born in Scotland, McIntosh moved to Georgia as a young man. His development in this country led him to sympathize with the Patriot cause, and he represented his parish in the Provincial Congress of 1775. In 1776, he was elected Brigadier General of the Continental troops of Georgia. In a power struggle within the patriot ranks, McIntosh engaged in a dual with fellow Patriot, Button Gwinnet. Both men were wounded, but Gwinnet mortally so.

To diffuse tensions within the rebel ranks, McIntosh was sent to George Washington's headquarters to represent the patriots in Georgia. At Valley Forge, Washington appointed McIntosh the command of the North Carolina Brigade, and in 1778 made him Brigadier General of the Continental Troops of Georgia.

McIntosh was taken prisoner by the British in his attempts to protect Charleston from invasion in 1780, and was not released until 1782. After the war, McIntosh served in a number of positions, including election to Congress in 1784. He was a member of the committee that welcomed George Washington to Savannah in 1791, and served the state throughout his lifetime until his death in 1806. He is buried in Colonial Cemetery.

The "Continentals" returned in two contingents in 1781, one under Lieutenant Colonel Henry "Light Horse Harry" Lee, a student of Pulaski's tactical cavalry support, the second under the new commander of the Southern department, Nathaniel Greene. After securing Augusta and defeating the Cherokee, they set the stage for the arrival of General "Mad" Anthony Wayne.

From the back: "General Lachlan McIntosh's Home 1782-1806 at 110 Oglethorpe Avenue East. First session of the Georgia Legislature held here after the evacuation of the city by the British 1782. General George Washington visited the house in 1791.

Circa 1940s; $3-5

"Mad" Anthony Wayne – who earned his reputation fighting alongside George Washington at Valley Forge, and the battles of Brandywine, Paoli, and other major northern fronts – was put in charge of Georgia operations. In 1782, Wayne launched a vigorous offensive in Georgia and, though outnumbered two to one, he easily advanced on the British stronghold of Savannah, which was promptly evacuated and officially surrendered.

In thanks, the Georgia legislature granted Wayne a plantation in the state, which he was later forced to sell because of financial problems.

Circa 1915; $5-8

Monument to Nathaniel Greene, with City Hall in the background. Greene and his son were eventually buried here.

City Hall, Green Monument, and Savannah Bank and Trust Co. Bldg., Savannah, Ga.

Cancelled 1917; $4-6

12

General Green's Headquarters.
Savannah, Ga.

17435

"General Green's Headquarters."

Circa 1930s; $3-5

The Civil War

To divide the southern Confederacy, President Lincoln ordered a blockade of Southern ports by the Union Navy. Without the heavy industry necessary to build a modern Navy, the Confederacy was helpless to resist. However, Georgia's coast, riddled with inlets, islands, hidden coves, and swamps provided many opportunities for blockade runners like the fictional hero of Gone With the Wind, Rhett Butler. Savannah, as Georgia's leading port, was an obvious goal of the invading Union forces. The city was well protected by Fort Pulaski, named for the Polish nobleman who fought the British in the Second Battle of Savannah in 1779. Sitting at the mouth of the Savannah River, across from Tybee Island, the fort was partially designed by a young Robert E. Lee after his graduation from West Point. It was considered invulnerable. Out of the range of Confederate guns, the Union landed a company of artillery in April 1862, but within range of their new, rifled cannons. After a night of Union bombardment during which the walls of the fort were breached, Confederate Col. Charles Olmstead surrendered the fort but Savannah did not fall until much later.

The "Squeezed Arch" at Fort Pulaski. From the back: "Fort Pulaski, on Cockspur Island, 17 miles from Savannah, is well preserved. Its walls are 7 to 11 feet thick, 32 feet high. Commanding both channels of the Savannah River, it was built to guard the approach to the port of Savannah."

Circa 1940s; $2-4

"Squeezed" Arch, Fort Pulaski

Sherman declared that "We can make war so terrible, and make them so sick of war that generations will pass away before they appeal to it again." With the blessing of President Abraham Lincoln and General Grant, Sherman began his infamous 300-mile march to the sea. With an army numbering nearly 100,000 men, he set out from Chattanooga in May of 1864 to crush the rebellion.

Sherman's army arrived in Savannah in two huge columns, devastation in their wake — plantations, towns, and railroads burned in a broad swath behind them. Sherman's troops quickly toppled a lightly manned Fort McAllister, which guarded the rear of the city. Seeing that he was about to be surrounded, General William Joseph Hardee evacuated the city by means of a pontoon bridge the night before Sherman's arrival. Leaving the lovely city intact, Sherman declared Savannah a Christmas gift for Lincoln. By May the following year, the war had ground to its end.

General Sherman's Headquarters on Madison Square. From the back: "In front of the City Exchange Sherman reviewed his army January 7th, 1865. This old weather beaten Colonial mansion of yellow stone was the headquarters of the conquering general."

Circa 1920; $5-8

The drawbridge entrance to Fort Pulaski over the moat in Fort Pulaski National Park.

Circa 1940s; $2-4

Additional early view of Sherman's Headquarters.

Cancelled 1906; $6-9

14

CONFEDERATE MONUMENT, SAVANNAH, GA.

One of many monuments erected to the Confederate Soldiers. This one, raised in 1875, stands in Forsyth Park. The inscription reads "Come from the four Winds O Breath and breathe upon these slain that they may live."

Circa 1920s; $4-6

CONFEDERATE MONUMENT, SAVANNAH, GA.

99022

A close-up of the Confederate Monument with the soldier facing north to repel the Yankee invaders.

Circa 1930s; $2-4

Fort Screven

Located 18 miles southeast of Savannah on Tybee Island, this fort enjoyed a long role in a system of coastal fortifications. Initially named Camp Graham, it was renamed in honor of James Screven, a Georgia Militia Brigadier General killed during the Revolutionary War. The Federal government obtained jurisdiction over the property in 1875, and the 20-gun fort was completed in 1901. The installation was the headquarters for Savannah's coastal defense, and played roles in Spanish-American War and both World Wars, and served as a base of recovery operations after a fire devastated the nearby town of Beaufort, South Carolina in 1907. After 1924 it was used as an artillery post and a deep-sea diving school. The War Department claimed Fort Screven surplus in 1944, and it was acquired by the town of Savannah Beach.

Bird's Eye View Fort Screven. Tybee Island near Savannah, Ga.

A bird's-eye view of Fort Screven.

Circa 1905; $8-10

POST THEATRE, FORT SCREVEN, SAVANNAH BEACH, GA.

The Post Theater at Fort Screven in Savannah Beach.

Circa 1940s; $2-4

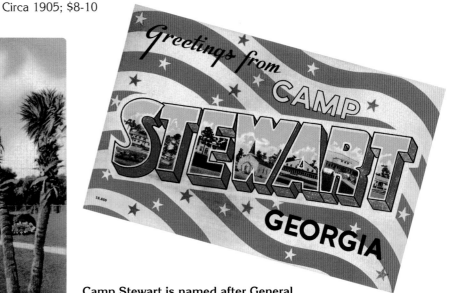

Camp Stewart is named after General Daniel Stewart a native of Liberty County Georgia and a Revolutionary War hero. The Camp currently encompasses 279,270 acres in Liberty, Long, Bryan, Evans, and Tattnall Counties.

Circa 1940s, $2-4

OFFICERS' QUARTERS, CAMP STEWART, SAVANNAH, GA.

The Camp Stewart Officers' Quarters. After World War II, the base's complement was severely depleted and only two officers were housed in these quarters.

Circa 1940s, $2-4

HOSPITAL AREA

CAMP STEWART, SAVANNAH, GEORGIA

A TYPICAL CHAPEL

HEADQUARTERS, CAMP STEWART
SAVANNAH, GEORGIA

The headquarters building at Camp Stewart. The Camp was established in 1940 to serve as an Anti-Aircraft Artillery Training Center.

Cancelled 1943, $2-4

The hospital area at Camp Stewart and one of the several chapels located on the base grounds.

Circa 1940s, $2-4

Fort Pulaski, located on Cockspur Island, was named after Count Casimir Pulaksi, a Polish General who died in the Second Battle of Savannah in 1779. The fort is also known for being the first military assignment of Robert E. Lee after his graduation from West Point in 1829.

Circa 1940s, $2-4

21—Aerial View of Fort Pulaski National Monument
Savannah, Georgia

ENTRANCE TO SAVANNAH AIR BASE, SAVANNAH, GA.

The front gate of the Savannah Air Base. No entrance was allowed without a pass.

Cancelled 1944, $2-4

HEADQUARTERS AREA, SAVANNAH AIR BASE, SAVANNAH, GA.

The Savannah Air Base was established in 1940. The base was originally named Hunter Municipal Airfield after Lt. Colonel Frank O'Driscoll Hunter, a World War I flying ace and native of Savannah. The base was renamed Savannah Air Base in 1941.

Cancelled 1941, $2-4

Savannah Air Base as seen from the eyes of the airmen stationed there.

Circa 1940s, $3-5

AERIAL CLOSEUP
SAVANNAH AIR BASE, SAVANNAH, GA.

The United States Marine Hospital built in 1907.

Circa 1940s, $2-4

The Chatham Artillery Armory on the south end of Forsyth Park.

Circa 1930s, $6-8

Plantation Life

The rich soil of the low country leant itself to the production of rice, indigo, and cotton, and Georgia finally bowed to economic pressure and became the last colony to legalize slavery in 1750. Slave labor provided a boon to the cultivation of crops, and farmer barons began cobbling the small farms that surrounded Savannah into larger plantations that fueled the region's economic growth. Savannah soon became a portal for thousands of Africans imported into the country, and the mix of African and European cultures combined to form the Geechee-Gullah culture unique to the Low Country of coastal Georgia and South Carolina.

The large plantations that grew up were often quite isolated and self-sustaining. Skilled slave labor was an important aspect, as each plantation would have its own blacksmith, carpenters, household help, and other tradesmen and specialists in addition to those who did the menial work of crop cultivation.

To spend their money, plantation owners and their families often kept residences in North Georgia and Savannah, and, of course, their cotton and other agricultural goods were brought here to be sold. Savannah soon rivaled Charleston to the north as a major commercial port. After the Civil War the world's cotton prices were often established on the steps of the Savannah Cotton Exchange, a grand building still in existence today.

The homes of the owners reflected the wealth accumulated in the flourishing agricultural industry, and plantation house tours have been a highlight for visitors to Savannah for as long as postcards have been produced. Savannah's more popular plantations are the Hermitage Plantation built by Henry McAlpin in 1819 and the Wormsloe Plantation established by Noble Jones in 1734. Devoted not only to agriculture, the Hermitage Plantation also housed an iron foundry, steam sawmill and brickworks. After a fire in 1820 devastated a majority of the wooden houses in Savannah, architect William Jay advocated constructing houses built of brick and supported and decorated by iron, which his friend Henry McAlpin was only too happy to supply from the Hermitage's foundry and brickworks. Meeting the demands of the populace allowed the plantation to prosper until McAlpin's death in 1851. Henry Ford purchased the big house in the 1930s and reconstructed it on the Ogeechee River.

Like the Hermitage, Wormsloe Plantation was not solely devoted to agricultural pursuits. An avid gardener, Noble Jones frequently experimented with different plants and maintained several gardens that were considered something of a local attraction. While the mansion at Wormsloe is still maintained as a private residence, the plantation grounds are open to the public.

5761. THE HERMITAGE, SAVANNAH, GA.   COPYRIGHT, 1900, BY DETROIT PHOTOGRAPHIC CO.

Henry McAlpin who came to Savannah from Scotland built the big house at Hermitage Plantation in 1819.

Circa 1910, $5-8

The slave huts at the Hermitage were built entirely from bricks made on the plantation.

Cancelled 1911, $5-8

The Hermitage big house like many of the buildings erected in Savannah during the 1820s was built in the Greek revival style.

Circa 1920s, $5-8

11527 THE HERMITAGE, SAVANNAH, GA.

COPR. DETROIT PUBLISHING CO.

The Hermitage Plantation spread along the south bank of the Savannah River.

Circa 1920s, $3-5

With the death of Henry McAlpin in 1851 the foundry at the Hermitage closed down and the rest of the plantation was abandoned after the Civil War.

Circa 1920s, $5-8

Brownie Gardens, one of the most beautiful in "Wormsloe", Savannah, Ga.

The Brownie Gardens are located on the privatley owned part of Wormsloe Plantation.

Cancelled 1944, $2-4

AZALEA POOL, WORMSLOE GARDENS, SAVANNAH, GA.-7

Noble Jones who sailed to Georgia from England with Oglethorpe in 1733 established Wormsloe Plantation.

Circa 1940, $2-4

THE PIER, WORMSLOE, NEAR SAVANNAH, GA.   114522

The Pier at Wormsloe. Between 1739 and 1745 Noble Jomes was responsible for protecting the inland waterway into Savannah from possible attacks by Spanish ships.

Circa 1940s, $5-8

In addition to its magnificent public gardens, Wormsloe is also known for its many oak trees planted throughout the plantation's grounds.

Circa 1930s, $2-4

SPANISH OAKS AT WORMSLOE, SAVANNAH, GA.   A-792

The City

Squares and Monuments

When Oglethorpe first envisioned the plan for Savannah, he designed for a city built around squares each of which would serve the colonists as stockyards, areas for meetings, and as a safe place to flee to in the event of an Indian attack. These squares still serve as public meeting places, and are the sites of numerous public and private events. They are popular destinations for tourists and full-time residents of Savannah who come to appreciate the beauty of the flora and the various monuments and fountains found in the squares. The first of these squares to be laid out was Johnson Square in 1733 named for the Royal Governor of South Carolina at the time of the colony's founding. The last square built in Savannah was Whitefield created in 1851 and named for the Reverend George Whitefield the minister who founded Bethesda Orphanage.

Being a city rich in history and prominent figures it would stand to reason that Savannah would possess a large number of monuments to commemorate the lives and deeds of these distinguished persons. Many of these monuments are centerpieces in Savannah's squares and serve to educate residents and visitors alike in the distinguished history of the city. The first monument in Savannah was a pyramid of stone erected in the middle of Wright Square over the grave of the Yamacraw Chieftain Tomochichi after his death in 1739. The monument is no longer there however a granite boulder to his memory was later placed in a different part of the square. Currently, the oldest standing monument is a pair of cannons captured at the Battle of Yorktown and presented to the Chatham Artillery by President George Washington after his visit to Savannah in 1791.

Located on Bull Street and facing Forsyth Park, this house was built in 1909 for Mills B. Lane and was designed by the design firm of Mowbray and Uffinger.

Circa 1940s, $2-4

Photo. only, Copyright 1904 by the Rotograph Co.
G 13689 Chippewa Square, Savannah, Ga.

Chippewa Square was established in 1815 to commemorate the American victory at the Battle of Chippewa during the War of 1812.

Cancelled 1909, $6-8

School children pose in Chippewa Square beside Civil War monuments since moved to Forsyth Park.

Circa, 1905, $5-8

Scenery

Called the "Forest City," Savannah is characterized by its abundant natural scenery. Stately live oaks (Georgia's State Tree) draped with curtains of Spanish moss are planted throughout the city and all of Savannah's squares and parks abound with colorful and fragrant flowers, bushes, and trees

Forysth Park was laid out in 1851 and stretches from Gaston Street to Park Avenue. The park contains the 1858 Forsyth Park Fountain, the Confederate Monument, and the Spanish American War Monument. The park was the vision of William Hodgson and was named for John Forsyth who was Governor of Georgia from 1827 to 1829 and Secretary of State from 1834 to 1841.

Bonaventure Cemetery was not intended to be a public park but was originally a private residence of the Mulryne and later the Tattnall family. There was a small family plot on the Bonaventure land but there was not an actual cemetery on the property until 1850. The cemetery was later placed under the administration of the Savannah Park and Tree Commission. Bonaventure attained stardom, however, via its inclusion in the bestselling book and subsequent movie, *Midnight in the Garden of Good and Evil* (1994) by John Berendt. And, because of the book, the cemetery is visited by hundreds who come to stroll through the grounds or take a picnic lunch beneath the two-hundred-year-old oaks dotted throughout the cemetery.

Not as large or famous as Bonaventure Cemetery, Colonial Cemetery is another idyllic escape advantageously located downtown, and very accessible to tourists. Colonial was closed to public burials in 1850 and is now used as a public park.

Forsyth Park was designed by William B. Hodgson and named for John Forsyth, a former governor of Georgia.

Circa 1900s, $3-5

FOUNTAIN IN FORSYTH PARK, SAVANNAH, GA.

The Forsyth Park Fountain was erected in
1858.

Cancelled 1918, $3-5

The Forsyth Park Fountain resembles the fountain located in the Place de la Concorde in Paris.

Circa 1910s, $3-5

The Promenade in Forsyth Park where many tourists and residents would stroll or sit on the benches to enjoy the scenery.

Cancelled 1905, $3-5

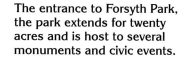

The entrance to Forsyth Park, the park extends for twenty acres and is host to several monuments and civic events.

Cancelled 1901, $4-6

Colonel John Mulryne first
settled Bonaventure in 1760
during the Royal Colony period.

Cancelled 1907, $3-5

Bonaventure Cemetery, Savannah, Ga.

Thousands of flowers like these azaleas are
planted throughout Forsyth Park creating a
vivid tapestry of colors.

Cancelled 1951, $2-4

Captain Peter Wiltberger transformed Bonaventure into a cemetery in 1850. The city then purchased the property in 1907 and placed it under the administration of the Park and Tree Commission.

Circa 1900s, $3-5

Bonaventure Cemetery enjoys great fame as one of the country's most beautiful burial grounds and many tourists and Savannahnians come to picnic and stroll through the cemetery's grounds.

Circa 1940s, $2-4

6A-H1883

The entrance to Bonaventure Cemetery on Bonaventure Road.

Cancelled 1951, $2-4

Naturalist John Muir once observed that Bonaventure contained "one of the most impressive assemblages of animal and plant creatures I have ever met."

Circa 1910s, $3-5

AVENUE IN BONAVENTURE CEMETERY, SAVANNAH, GA.

Another view of the entrance to Bonaventure Cemetery.

Circa 1910s, $3-5

Many of the trees in Bonaventure Cemetery are over two hundred years old.

Circa 1930s, $3-5

One of the many
beautiful private
gardens found
throughout Savannah.

Circa 1910s, $2-4

Opened in 1750, the Colonial Park
Cemetery was the second public burial
ground in Savannah.

Cancelled 1924, $3-5

Live Oaks Draped with Moss, Savannah, Ga.—68

A resolution passed by the Georgia General Assembly in 1937 made the live oak the official tree of the state.

Cancelled 1929, $3-5

Oak trees like this one are often pictured on post cards and are greatly admired by visiting tourists.

Cancelled 1935, $2-4

OLD OAK IN SAVANNAH HOSPITAL GROUNDS, SAVANNAH, GA.—79

View Along Shore, Isle of Hope, by Moonlight, Savannah, Ga.

The Isle of Hope, a resort community "on the salts" as the locals say was settled in 1737, not long after Savannah was settled.

Circa 1910s, $2-4

Victory Drive is the longest palm-lined drive in the world and its palms memorialize soldiers who died in World War I.

Circa 1940s, $2-4

Azaleas in Bloom Along Beautiful Victory Drive, Savannah, Georgia

AC-832   AN ALLURING HIGHWAY SCENE DOWN SOUTH

A highway in Georgia lined with live oaks draped with Spanish moss.

Cancelled 1916, $2-4

PALMS AND OLEANDERS, HIGHWAY TO SAVANNAH BEACH, GA.—57

The highway leading from Savannah to Savannah Beach and Tybee Island is the longest avenue of palms in the world.

Circa 1940s, $2-4

The Cherokee rose, the State Flower of Georgia.

Circa 1950s, $3-5

Citizens of Savannah take the afternoon to enjoy the scenery in Forsyth Park.

Circa 1910s, $5-8

The entrance to Forsyth Park, also the promenade that leads to the famous Forsyth Park Fountain.

Circa 1940s, $3-5

Streets

The streets of Savannah are so beautiful that they have inspired artists and photographers, as attested by these postcards. Residential streets are lined with live oaks, magnolias, and palm trees, divided by tree lawns and medians planted with azaleas and other flowers. Even commercial streets like Broughton were studded with Colonial, Greek revival, and Victorian architecture.

A view of Broughton Street at night.

Cancelled 1952, $4-6

From the 1880s to the 1960s, Broughton Street was the retail center of Savannah.

Cancelled 1920, $8-12

BROUGHTON STREET, EAST FROM BARNARD STREET, SAVANNAH, GA.

Looking east on Broughton Street, a person can see the sheer number of stores and businesses that gave the street its reputation as the retail heart of the city.

Cancelled 1919, $8-10

LOOKING WEST ON BROUGHTON STREET, SAVANNAH, GA.—86

Cars line both sides of Broughton Street waiting for their drivers and passengers to return from shopping.

Circa 1931, $8-10

Broughton Street facing east and showing the "Main Buisness District" of Savannah.

Circa 1930s, $6-8

Broughton Street, Looking East, showing Main Business District, Savannah, Ga.

Corner Bull and Broughton Street,
Showing National and Germania Bank Buildings at Night,
Savannah, Ga.

Broughton Street, Savannah, Ga.

A glimpse of
Broughton Street
with wagons and
streetcars crowding
the street.

Circa 1900s, $8-10

The National and Germania Bank Building
located at the corner of Broughton and Bull
Streets. The Germania Bank Building was
designed by Henrik Wallin and Hyman Witcover
and has since been demolished.

Circa 1911, $6-9

Bull Street, Savannah, Ga.

Bull Street was named for Colonel William Bull, a South Carolinian who assisted James Oglethorpe in laying out the city.

Circa 1900s, $9-12

Bull Street as seen from the north end of the street looking south.

Cancelled 1916, $8-10

Bull Street looking South, Savannah, Ga.

S-12— BULL STREET LOOKING NORTH FROM WRIGHT SQUARE, SAVANNAH, GA.

**With so many trees it is easy to see why
Savannah is called the "Forest City".**

Circa 1930s, $8-10

**Looking north on
Bull Street.**

Cancelled 1912, $9-12

Bull Street, looking North, Savannah, Ga.

47

South Broad Street was renamed Oglethorpe Avenue in honor of the city's founder.

Cancelled 1907, $8-10

The favorite promenade in Savannah stretches from City Hall to Forsyth Park.

Cancelled 1910, $9-12

"The New Savannah River Bridge" connected the city of Savannah with Coastal South Carolina.

Circa 1940s, $5-6

SAVANNAH VIADUCT, SAVANNAH, GA.

The Savannah Viaduct is 3,200 feet long and leads from U.S. Highway 17 into Savannah.

Circa 1940s, $5-6

Bird's-eye View from Top of Georgia State Savings Bank Bldg., Savannah, Ga.

Washington Avenue, Savannah, Ga.

A "bird's-eye view" of Savannah from the roof of the Georgia State Savings Bank Building, now Wachovia Bank.

Cancelled 1918, $8-10

Washington Avenue like many Savannah streets is lined with fragrant flowers and trees.

Cancelled 1943, $2-4

Liberty Street, has an impressive wide median.

Cancelled 1907, $8-10

The entrance to Ardsley Park, one of the first automobile suburbs built in Savannah.

Circa 1930s, $7-8

3— PALM-LINED VICTORY DRIVE, SAVANNAH, GA.

6A-H1882

Another close-up view of "palm-lined" Victory Drive.

Circa 1940s, $2-4

ESTELL AVENUE, SAVANNAH, GA.

Estill Avenue, later renamed Victory Drive, like many of the avenues in Savannah is lined with palms.

Cancelled 1924, $7-8

SKYLINE VIEW, SAVANNAH, GA.—77

A skyline view of Savannah "where beauty, romance, and history walk hand in hand with buisness and enterprise."

Circa 1940s, $7-8

Eugene Talmadge Memorial Bridge
Savannah, Georgia

The Eugene Talmadge Bridge was 6,304 feet long and was built as a memorial to Eugene Talmadge, a former Governor of Georgia.

Circa 1950s, $3-5

BIRD'S EYE VIEW OF BUSINESS SECTION, SAVANNAH, GA.

11

A "bird's-eye view" of Savannah's Business Section.

Cancelled 1930, $4-6

Liberty Street as
seen looking east
from Bull Street.

Circa 1900s, $7-8

Interesting examples of Savannah's architecture can be found on Bull Street.

Circa 1910, $8-10

Gaston Street named after William Gaston who worked with the artist John
James Audubon, and served as a local agent for his book *Birds of America*.

Circa 1910s, $3-5

A view of some of the elegant Victorian style homes on the north end of Bull Street.

Circa 1900s, $5-8

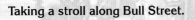
Taking a stroll along Bull Street.

Cancelled 1908, $8-10

10576   BULL STREET, SAVANNAH, GA.

COPYRIGHT, 1907, BY
DETROIT PUBLISHING CO.

56

Government Buildings and Schools

Savannah has long been known for its commitment to style and beauty. One only has to look at the hundreds of trees that dot the city and the many elegant Greek revival houses to understand that Savannah residents take the personal appearance of their city very seriously. Not content with the drab utilitarian government buildings found in other cities, the people of Savannah took it upon themselves to design and build public buildings that combined usefulness and functionality with a sense of architectural style and sophistication. Architects like William Gibbons Preston who designed the Chatham County Courthouse, William Aiken who designed the old Post Office Building, William Jay, the designer of the building that would eventually become the Telfair Academy of Arts and Sciences, and Hyman W.

Witcover strove to design buildings that reflected this view. The results were many buildings that functioned well as government buildings while displaying the sense of architectural sophistication and beauty for which Savannah is so well known. Surprising enough none of these architects were originally from Savannah but had moved here from other cities.

In addition to its many tourist attractions, Savannah boasts several fine colleges and universities. Savannah State University, formerly Georgia State Industrial College for Colored Youth, the oldest public black university in the state of Georgia. Founded in 1890, the college moved to its current location in Savannah from Athens, Georgia in 1891, Armstrong Junior College, currently Armstrong Atlantic State University, and the Savannah College of Art and Design, which has been responsible for the restoration of many of Savannah's historic buildings.

Union Station in Savannah offered the "finest passenger service in the country."

Cancelled 1942, $3-5

57

The Chatham County Courthouse was built in 1889 by William Gibbons Preston. Its construction refelcted the fad for Romanesque revival and English Romantic architectural styles in Savannah.

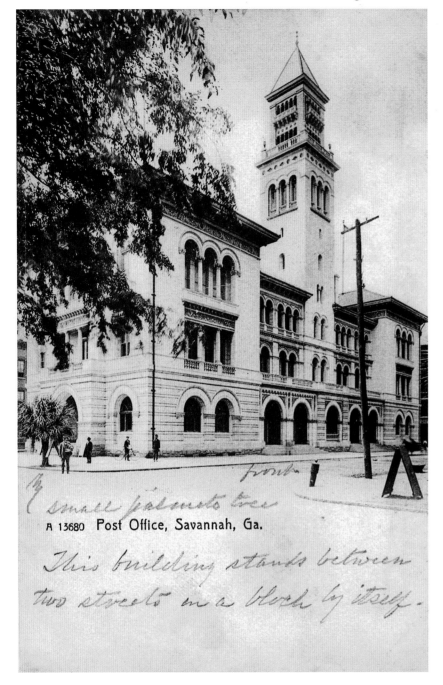

The Savannah Post office was designed by William Aiken and built in 1898.

Circa 1940s, $6-8

Statues of Phidias, Raphael, Rubens, Michelangelo, and Rembrandt welcome visitors to the Telfair Academy of Arts and Sciences.

Circa 1940s, $4-6

The Federal Building. Savannah, Ga.

An addition to the Post Office was added on in 1931. James A. Wetmore, the supervising architect, was particularly careful to construct the addition in the same style as the original building.

Circa 1940s, $6-8

TELFAIR ACADEMY OF ARTS AND SCIENCES, SAVANNAH, GA.

William Jay, the architect who designed homes for many of Savannah's prominent families, designed and oversaw the construction of the residence that was to become the Telfair Academy of Arts and Sciences. The building was donated to the Georgia Historical Society in 1875. It is the oldest public art museum in the South.

Circa 1925, $3-5

UNION DEPOT, SAVANNAH, GA.

Visitors arriving and departing Savannah cluster around the entrance of the Union Depot in Savannah.

Circa 1940s, $4-6

Naval Stores Dock, Savannah, Ga.

The Naval Storage Dock in Savannah. In addition to being a city of great beauty, Savannah was also well known for its role in the national and international shipping trades.

Circa 1910s, $8-10

Like many of the public buildings in Savannah, Union Station combined functionality and architectural style. It was demolished to make way for Interstate I-16.

Circa 1940s, $4-6

The United States Marine Hospital in Savannah, dedicated to Marines from Savannah who served in the Spanish-American War and World War I.

Circa 1940s, $6-8

BETHESDA HOME FOR BOYS, SAVANNAH, GA.—106

Chatham Artillery, Savannah, Ga.

Founded in 1740 by the Reverend George Whitefield, the Bethesda Home for Boys is the oldest operating orphanage in the United States.

Cancelled 1935, $6-8

The Chatham Artillery formerly housed a pair of cannons given to the unit by George Washington. They were fired on special occasions to welcome distinguished visitors to Savannah.

Circa 1940s, $6-8

U. S. COURT HOUSE AND POST OFFICE, SAVANNAH, GA.

P. C. KROPP, PUBL., MILWAUKEE. NO. 1265.

No. 475   AERIAL VIEW OF SAVANNAH AIR BASE—SAVANNAH, GA.

A "pilot's eye view" of the Savannah Air Base.

Cancelled 1941, $5-7

Another view of the Savannah Court House and Post Office.

Circa 1900s, $6-8

City Hall, Savannah, Ga.

Hyman W. Witcover who designed many of Savannah's public and private buildings designed the Savannah City Hall.

Circa 1920s, $6-8

3590 Chatham County Court House, Savannah, Ga.

Another view of the Chatham County Court House.

Circa 1900s, $6-8

11 U. S. POST OFFICE, SAVANNAH, GA.

6A-H1890

As the oldest city in Georgia, Savannah boasts many beautiful buildings such as the Post Office Building pictured here.

Cancelled 1939, $2-4

Fort Pulaski itself is 1,580 feet in circumference and is comprised of solid brick walls seven to eleven feet thick.

Cancelled 1955, $3-5

13—Ramparts of Historic Fort Pulaski, Showing Atlantic Ocean in Distance
Savannah Beach, Georgia

S-10—Savannah High School, Savannah, Ga.

Like many of the buildings in Savannah, the Savannah High School sports Grecian Columns and is built out of brick.

Cancelled 1944, $3-5

Armstrong Junior College in Savannah was named for George Ferguson Armstrong whose family donated his house to the college in 1935.

Cancelled 1949, $3-5

The Barnard Street School was built in 1901 in the Egyptian Revival style and is currently owned by the Savannah College of Art and Design.

Circa 1900s, $6-8

Churches

Oglethorpe's plan for the city of Savannah included the allotment of trust lots on the east and west sides of each square for public buildings. The first church built on one of these squares was Christ Church. As the colony grew, so did the number of churches and the rich religious tradition that came along with them.

From its founding days Savannah, and Georgia as well, has been a place of religious diversity. Evangelical Lutherans from Salzburg, Austria, Moravians from Germany, Jews from Portugal, English Anglicans, and Scottish Presbyterians were among the colony's first settlers. Savannah was also the site of the first African-American Baptist Church in the United States, founded in 1788. Despite this atmosphere of religious tolerance, Catholics were originally forbidden from publically worshipping until the end of the 1700s.

Perhaps the most famous religious figures to live in Savannah were John Wesley and his brother Charles, who both spent some time preaching at the Christ Church where John also taught the first Sunday school in North America. According to local legend, John Wesley soon became unpopular for walking around the colony, recording the sins he saw and the names of those committing them and then reporting them from his church's pulpit.

St. John's Episcopal Church was designed in 1853 by Calvin Otis and was dedicated that same year.

Circa 1940s, $3-5

The Catholic Cathedral of St. John the Baptist was built in 1872-1876 by architect, Francis Baldwin.

Circa 1900s, $6-8

The Cathedral of St. John the Baptist as seen from the former home of Juliette Gordon Low, the founder of the Girl Scouts.

Circa 1940s, $2-4

Christopher Murphy a local artist, created some of the murals inside the Cathedral of St. John the Baptist.

Circa 1920s, $5-7

19—Cathedral of St. John the Baptist
Savannah, Georgia

The Cathedral of St. John the Baptist is
one of the largest Roman Catholic
Cathedrals in the South.

Cancelled 1952, $2-4

The Sacred Heart Church and Parsonage, one of the many elegant
churches found in Savannah.

Circa 1900s, $6-8

SAVANNAH, Ga. St. Patrick's Church.

St. Patrick's Church in Savannah, now demolished.

Circa 1900s, $6-8

Wesley Monumental Methodist Church, Savannah, Ga.

Salzbergers from Central Europe founded the Ebenezer Church in the early colonial days of Savannah.

Cancelled 1936, $2-4

The Wesley Monumental Methodist Church was built in 1876 and is dedicated to John and Charles Wesley, the founders of the movement which later evolved into the Methodist denomination.

Circa 1900s, $6-8

The land on which Christ Church stands was originally set aside in 1733 Oglethorpe for the first church to be built in the colony.

Circa 1940s, $4-6

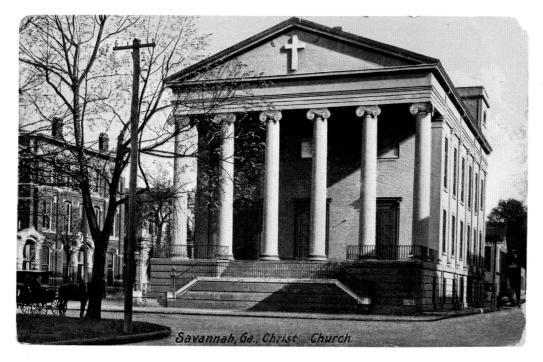

Savannah, Ga., Christ Church.

The first church service held in the colony was was held on this spot. The first building built on the Christ Church site was completed in 1750.

Cancelled 1906, $6-8

The Reverend John Wesley, who came to Savannah on Oglethorpe's second voyage, taught the first Sunday school class taught in North America.

Cancelled 1905, $4-6

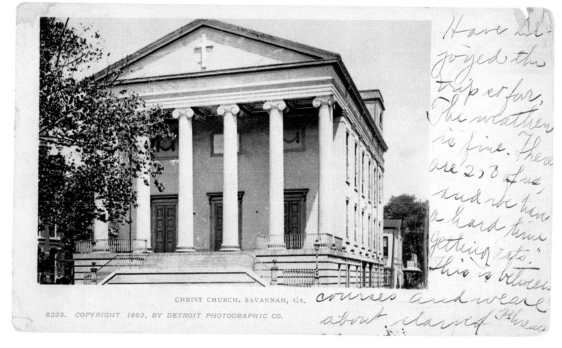

CHRIST CHURCH, SAVANNAH, GA.

6329. COPYRIGHT 1902, BY DETROIT PHOTOGRAPHIC CO.

When the Savannah Methodist Congregation became too small to meet in the Wesley Chapel on Oglethorpe Avenue the Trinity Methodist Church was constructed in 1850.

Circa 1940s, $5-6

The Independent Presbyterian Church was founded as a branch of the Church of Scotland in 1755. The current building is a reproduction of the original building of 1819 that was destroyed by a fire in 1889. Woodrow Wilson married Ellen Axson, his first wife, in the manse behind the Independent Presbyterian Church in 1885.

Circa 1940s, $2-4

Midway Church, Midway,
Erected in 1792 on U. S. Highway 17,
South of Savannah, Ga.

The congregation came to Georgia in 1752 and the Midway Church was created in 1792 and is currently located south of Savannah on U.S. Highway 17.

Circa 1940s, $2-4

The present Christ Church building was designed by James Hamilton Couper and constructed in 1838 and is the fourth building to occupy that site.

Cancelled 1953, $2-4

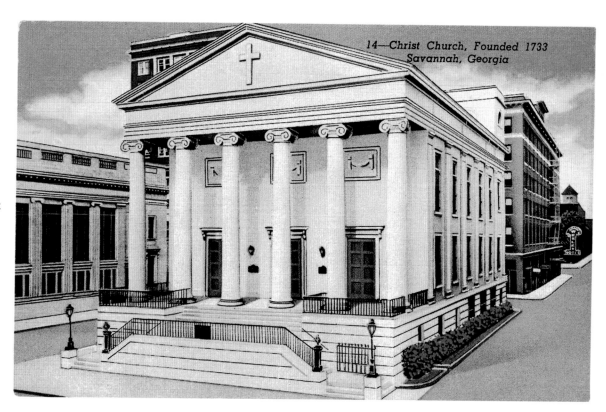

14—Christ Church, Founded 1733
Savannah, Georgia

The interior of the Cathedral of St. John the Baptist. The windows in the Cathedral were imported from Innsbruck, Austria.

Cancelled 1911, $6-8

Thirteen members of the Independent Presbyterian Church founded the First Presbyterian Church of Savannah Georgia in 1827. The First Presbyterian Church was the first church in the city to be affiliated with the Presbytery of Georgia.

Circa 1900s, $5-7

John Holden Greene, an architect from Rhode Island, designed the Independent Presbyterian Church building. The building itself is modeled after St. Martin's-in-the-Field in London.

Circa 1920s, $6-8

Banks

After the invention of the cotton gin, the export of cotton became Savannah's main industry. The industry made some of the citizens of Savannah very wealthy.

Several of the banks built in Savannah were designed by the New York architectural firm of Mowbray and Uffinger. As with the public buildings and private homes in Savannah, the bank buildings were built with an idea that they should be pleasing to the eye as well as functional. The Savannah Bank & Trust Company building, for example, was built in three levels after a Greek tripartite style and the Citizens and Southern Bank building was designed to match the Christ Church. Built in the late 1800s and early 1900s, many bank buildings now hold a proud place in Savannah's architectural heritage.

The Greene Monument and the National Bank of Savannah Building as seen from Johnson Square.

Cancelled 1919, $6-8

The Citizen's Bank Building was designed in 1912 by the architectural firm of Mowbray and Uffinger.

Cancelled 1912, $6-8

The National Bank of Savannah.

Circa 1900s, $6-8

Like many of the buildings in Savannah, the Chatham Bank (now Southern Bank) was built in a Classical revival style.

Cancelled 1913, $6-8

A view of Savannah as seen from the top of the Georgia
State Savings Bank Building, now Wachovia Bank.

Circa 1920s, $7-9

Mowbray and Uffinger the
same architects who
designed the Citizens and
Southern National Bank
and the Citizens Bank in
Savannah designed the
Savannah Bank & Trust
Company.

Circa 1920s, $6-8

Hyman Witcover, the architect of the Germania Bank was one of the architects who worked on the construction of the Astor Hotel in New York City. The building has since been demolished.

Circa 1920s, $6-8

Designed in a Greek tripartite scheme, the Savannah Bank and Trust Company Building blends in well with Savannah's classic architectural style.

Circa 1920s, $6-8

The Citizens and Southern Bank was built in 1907 and stylistically mirrored the nearby Christ Church.

Circa 1920s, $6-8

The Savannah Banking Center, right across Bay Street from the Cotton Exchange.

Circa 1920s, $4-6

Houses and Buildings of Note

Some of the finest examples of Savannah's architecture can be found in its residences, with excellent examples of Greek Revival, English Regency, Georgian, Federal, and Italianate style houses. Some of the historic houses in Savannah's downtown Historic District were built by local builders John H. Ash and Isaiah Davenport, both heads of the Savannah Mechanics Association. Wealthy residents of Savannah turned to "out of town" architects to design and build their houses. One such architect was William Jay, who was brought from England by a group of cotton merchants in 1817. Jay designed several buildings including the Owens-Thomas House, the Scarbrough House, and the original part of the Telfair Academy Museum of Art.

However, architecture is not the only thing that makes Savannah's houses so distinct. As a city with a fascinating history, many of Savannah's houses and other buildings of note have histories connected with that of the city and with the wider world. The Pirates' House, some have claimed was once a buccaneer tavern and is now a famous restaurant. Other buildings of note include the Low House, the birthplace of Juliette Gordon Low, who founded the Girl Scouts of America, and the Old Pink House, said to be the oldest brick house in Savannah and now a fine restaurant.

Old Pirates' House Garden and Trustees' Herb House, Savannah, Ga.

The gardens of the Pirates' House and the Herb House. This restaurant is one of the most historic restaurants in Savannah.

Circa 1940s, $2-4

The Pirates' House is said to be the site where the buccaneer, Captain Flint, died in the novel *Treasure Island*.

Cancelled 1985, $3-5

Florence Martus, Savannah's "Waving Girl," lived with her brother for forty years in this house on Elba Island.

Circa 1940s, $3-5

Pulaski House was a hotel owned by Captain Peter Wiltberger, who was also one of the original owners of Bonaventure Cemetery.

Circa 1920s, $6-8

The Old Pink House was built in 1789 by James Habersham Jr. and is said to be the oldest brick house in Georgia.

Circa 1940s, $2-4

The Low House was built by Andrew Low in 1849 and was the home of his daughter-in-law Juliette Gordon Low who founded the Girl Scouts of America.

Cancelled 1937, $5-7

THE LOW HOUSE,
SAVANNAH, GA.—120

The carriage house behind the Low House was the first headquarters of a Girl Scout chapter in America and is still used by the local chapter.

Circa 1930s, $2-4

In this house on Halloween night in 1860 was born Juliette Gordon Low, founder of the Girl Scouts.

Circa 1940s, $5-7

The Old Pink House has served many functions. It was the home of colonial leader James Habersham, the headquarters of the Savannah branch of the First Bank of the United States, and the headquarters of Union General York, a subordinate of General Sherman at the end of the Civil War.

Circa 1957, $2-4

The Georgian Tea Room (1929)
In "The Old Pink House" (1771)
23 Abercorn Street
Savannah, Georgia

Knights of Pythias Castle Hall, Savannah, Ga.

The Knights of Pythia Castle Hall, the Knights are the first American Order to be chartered by Congress. The Savannah Lodge wass one of many Pythian Lodges found throughout the United States and Canada. The building has since been demolished.

Circa 1920s, $6-8

Owens-Thomas House
Savannah, Ga.

The Owens-Thomas house has been called "the most perfect example of English Regency in America." Since 1954 it has been open to the public.

Circa 1940, $2-4

Early American kitchen in the Telfair Museum recalls the earlier kitchens of Savannah.

Circa 1940s, $5-6

EARLY AMERICAN KITCHENS   TELFAIR ACADEMY   SAVANNAH GA.

Industry

When the colony of Georgia was first founded in 1733 the aims of the Trustees were to produce silk, indigo, and wine. In 1750, the ban on slavery was lifted and rice cultivation became Savannah's primary industry, driven by slave labor. Then in 1793 the industrial face of Savannah was changed forever by the invention of the cotton gin by Eli Whitney. The cotton gin mechanically separated cotton fibers from cotton seeds. The old process was done by hand and took too much time and energy to make the growing and exportation of cotton profitable. The cotton gin was the device that made cotton "King." Ships from Europe and other parts of America soon flocked to Savannah to fill their cargo space with bales of cotton. During the reign of King Cotton, Savannah was the biggest cotton port on the Atlantic Ocean and the second largest exporter of cotton in the world. Two million bales passed through the port of Savannah every year and the Savannah Cotton Exchange was the economic center of the city.

Than after World War I Savannah's fortunes began to change, a boll weevil epidemic swept through Georgia and by the 1920s half of the state's cotton crop was destroyed. The city entered a depression, deepened even more by the stock market crash of 1929 that brought the rest of the nation to its knees. President Franklin D. Roosevelt and the New Deal helped revive Savannah, and new industries, particularly the paper industry, helped the city to prosper again.

With the invention of the cotton gin by Eli Whitney in 1793, the economy of Savannah was transformed and cotton became its primary export.

Cancelled 1931, $2-4

BIRD'S EYE VIEW OF RIVER FRONT, SHOWING STEAM SHIP TERMINALS, SAVANNAH, GA.

A "bird's eye view" of the Savannah River front, showing the terminals where steamships docked.

Cancelled 1923, $5-8

AEROPLANE VIEW, SAVANNAH, GA.—88

The harbor in Savannah was thirty-two feet deep and was open for navigation by steamers year-round.

Circa 1940s, $7-10

River Scene, Savannah, Ga.

Another view of the Savannah River.

Cancelled 1906, $8-10

BIRD'S EYE VIEW OF "SEABOARD" DOCKS, SAVANNAH HARBOR, SAVANNAH, GA.

An aerial view of the "Seaboard" Docks on Hutchinson Island.

Circa 1910s, $8-10

Dockhands wait for arriving ships in the shade along the Savannah River.

Circa 1900s, $9-11

Savannah boasted the largest port in the Southeastern United States.

Circa 1910s, $9-11

The Savannah River

SAVANNAH, GEORGIA

Down on the wharf.

The masts of a schooner poke above the roof of a warehouse on the Savannah River front.

Circa 1900s, $9-11

A view of Savannah harbor overlooking various buildings along the western harbor front.

Cancelled 1918, $10-12

SAVANNAH HARBOR LOOKING WEST, SAVANNAH, GA.

5758. DOWN THE RIVER, SAVANNAH, GA.

Known as "Factor's Row" this section of the Savannah River front contained many offices and warehouses of companies involved in the cotton trade.

Circa 1900, $9-11

A view of the Savannah harbor, looking west from City Hall.

Circa 1910s, $10-12

Savannah Harbor, West from City Hall, Savannah, Ga.

COPR. DETROIT PUBLISHING CO.

70245 RIVER FROM CITY HALL, SAVANNAH, GA.

A view of "Factor's Row" as seen from City Hall.

Cancelled 1920, $10-12

Ocean steamers along the Savannah River. The city was and is a frequent destination for both cargo and pleasure ships.

Circa 1920s, $9-12

Ocean Steamer on Savannah River, Savannah, Ga.

Workers stroll through one of Savannah's many cotton yards toward home at the end of their shifts.

Circa 1930s, $8-10

COTTON SCENE, C. OF GA. O. S. S. CO'S. YARDS, SAVANNAH, GA.

26. Cotton Yards, Cotton Ready for Shipment.

Bales of cotton await shipment. Cotton from Savannah was shipped throughout the United States and the rest of the world.

Cancelled 1915, $8-10

14914—*Naval Stores Wharf, SAVANNAH, Ga.*

A lone worker poses amidst the endless sea of barrels on the Naval Stores Wharf.

Circa 1910s, $9-11

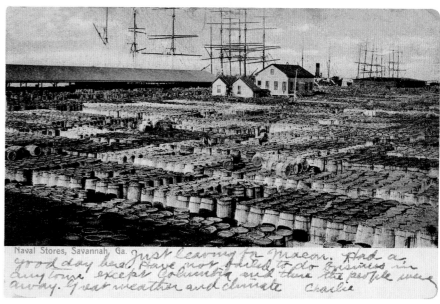

Naval Stores, Savannah, Ga.

At the time, Savannah was one of the largest naval stores ports for in the world.

Cancelled 1907, $8-10

The Cotton Yard of the Central of Georgia Railroad. Cotton from Georgia and other Southern states was often shipped by railroad to Savannah.

Circa 1920s, $9-11

A view of the Cotton Wharves. From here cotton bales were shipped to various warehouses throughout the world.

Cancelled 1916, $4-6

Savannah was the largest cotton seaport on the Atlantic Ocean and the second largest in the world.

Circa 1940s, $10-12

Cotton Shipping, Savannah, Ga.—87

Ocean Steamer leaving Savannah, Ga.

The S.S. *City of Macon* took passengers to and from New York.

Circa 1940s, $9-11

97

Another view of the Savannah River and the buildings on "Factor's Row" looking west from Bull Street.

Circa 1920s, $10-12

Cotton Exchange, Savannah, Ga.

Thank you for the shut-in magazines. When I finish with them will pass them on to others. Glad you are having a pleasant summer. W.W.

The Cotton Exchange, the palace when "King Cotton" ruled in Savannah. The building itself was erected in 1887.

Cancelled 1907, $8-10

Another view of "Factor's Row", also known as "Cotton Row" and the "Seaboard" Cotton Docks.

Circa 1930s, $7-9

THE STEAMSHIP "SAVANNAH"

****

The "Savannah" sailed from the port of Savannah, Georgia, on May 22, 1819 for Liverpool and took 27 days for the voyage.

****

The Steamship Savannah was the first steamship to cross the Atlantic Ocean.

Cancelled 1937, $6-7

COTTON SHIPPING AT SAVANNAH, GA.

A-796

At one time over two million bales of cotton were shipped annually from Savannah.

Circa 1920s, $8-10

Cotton Loading, Savannah, Ga.

Cotton bales were floated out on a barge and then loaded onto a waiting steamer.

Circa 1910s, $8-10

AERIAL VIEW

PLANT OF SAVANNAH SUGAR REFINING CORPORATION

An aerial view of the Savannah Sugar Refining Corporation Plant located six miles northeast of the city on U.S. Highway 17.

Circa 1940s, $7-9

An open-air farmers' market, Farmers would bring their produce to Savannah and sell it in markets like these.

Circa 1910s, $8-10

THE MARKET, SAVANNAH, GA.

Aerial View of World's Largest Integrated Kraft Container Plant, Savannah, Ga.

Built on the site of the Hermitage Plantation, the Union Bag and Paper Corporation plant was one of the largest of its kind in the world.

Circa 1940s, $6-8

Bird's Eye View of Business Section, Savannah, Ga.

A "bird's eye view" of Savannah's business section overlooking offices, warehouses and a good mix of residences.

Cancelled 1915, $8-10

The "Savannah" was the first steam-powered vessel to cross the Atlantic Ocean. It departed Savannah May 22nd, 1819 and arrived in Liverpool, England June 20th, twenty-seven days later.

Cancelled 1944, $6-7

Shipping Scene, Savannah, Ga.

Another "shipping scene" where paddle steamers wait alongside the riverfront for cargo.

Cancelled 1917, $9-10

Savannah River West from Bull St., Savannah, Ga.

Three-masted schooners docked at Savannah harbor.

Circa 1910s, $6-8

Tourism

Sports

The Savannah area was home to many kinds of sports and leisure activities in the early 1900s. A casino in the nearby town of Thunderbolt offered a wide variety of amusements ranging from gambling to nightly motion picture shows. The Savannah Yacht Club hosted annual regattas, usually in the month of May, on the Wilmington River. Motorboat races were also held by the club in the earlier part of the twentieth century. For those who were not nautically inclined, Savannah also played host to the Savannah Grand Prize and the Vanderbilt Cup Prize. There was also the game of golf to be pursued at the Savannah Golf Club.

Thunderbolt Casino, near Savannah, Ga.

The Savannah Electric Company built the Thunderbolt Casino in 1895 in the hopes that it would increase the number of people riding its streetcars to Thunderbolt. The Thunderbolt Casino also to showcased the versatility of electricity with lights, fans, and motion picture projectors.

Cancelled 1917, $6-8

The Savannah Yacht Clubhouse was built on the banks of the Wilmington River in the 1880s.

Circa 1910s, $7-8

Savannah Yacht Club, Savannah, Ga.

The Casino, Thunderbolt, Savannah, Ga.

The Thunderbolt Casino was also the first place in Savannah where silent motion pictures were shown.

Circa 1900s, $6-8

A side view of the Savannah Yacht Club. In the back of the clubhouse, the club maintained a pavilion called Pedrick's Pavilion where members could dock their yachts.

Circa 1900s, $7-8

Savannah Yacht Club, Thunderbolt, near SAVANNAH, Ga.

The Band Stand, in Grounds of Casino, Thunderbolt, Savannah, Ga.

The bandstand at the Thunderbolt Casino was the site of concerts and dances.

Circa 1900s, $7-8

Casino at Thunderbolt Savannah Ga - Moonlight.

The grounds of the Thunderbolt Casino included a pond where visitors could feed tame ducks.

Cancelled 1907, $4-5

Savannah Grand Prize and
Vanderbilt Cup Race 1911
Auto Course, Along White Bluff Road.

SAVANNAH GOLF CLUB, SAVANNAH, GA.

The old Savannah Golf Club, one of the many golf clubs and courses found in the area around the city.

Cancelled 1926, $4-6

The first auto races in Savannah were held on the 18th and 19th of March, 1908. An automobile course along White Bluff Road played host to the Savannah Grand Prize and the Vanderbuilt Cup Race in 1911.

Circa 1910s, $3-5

Yacht Club House, near Savannah, Ga.

During 1886, twenty-four yachts were registered at the Savannah Yacht Club and the price of annaul membership was ten dollars a year.

Cancelled 1909, $6-8

Tightrope bicyclers dangle entertained the amused spectators at the Thunderbolt Casino. Performances like this were just one of the types of free entertainment provided for casino guests.

Circa 1900s, $6-8

Casino Thunderbolt, Near Savannah, Ga.

Hotels

The Hostess City has long been home to luxury hotels and accommodations for tourists and business travelers alike. The first hotels in Savannah were inns and taverns built during the colonial period to serve visiting merchants and sailors. As the city grew in importance, the number of hotels multiplied, and grew more elaborate. In 1851, Mary L. Marshall built the Marshall House, which became the first of many grand hotels to call Savannah home.

The Hotel Desoto a "premier Southern hotel."

Circa 1930s, $6-8

The Hotel Desoto, one of Savannah's finest Hotels, the building pictured here was demolished in 1966 and rebuilt as the Desoto Hilton Hotel. Henry Urban, the same architect who designed the Beth Eden Baptist Church, designed the first Hotel Desoto building.

Circa 1920s, $6-8

The Hotel Desoto possessed 8,900 square feet of porch space.

Circa 1910s, $6-8

DESOTO HOTEL, SAVANNAH, GA.   A-763

A side view of the Hotel Desoto.

Circa 1910s, $6-8

16—Hotel De Soto,
Savannah, Georgia

The Hotel Desoto was "Savannah's leading, most modern hotel."

Circa 1940s, $4-6

HOTEL DE SOTO, SAVANNAH.

H. Hymes, Art Store, Savannah, Ga.

The Hotel Desoto was so large that it covered an entire city block.

Cancelled 1904, $6-8

Dining Room of The De Soto, Savannah, Ga.

The Dining Room in the Hotel Desoto where fine dining was available.

Cancelled 1920, $7-9

DESOTO HOTEL, SAVANNAH, GA.—132

A hotel like the Hotel Desoto was "a great attraction for tourists and pleasure seekers."

Circa 1940s, $4-6

Tropical foliage surrounded the court and swimming pool of the Hotel Desoto.

Cancelled 1928, $5-7

COURT AND SWIMMING POOL, HOTEL DE SOTO, SAVANNAH, GA.

A view of the court of the Hotel Desoto, featuring the pool and the miniature golf course.

Circa 1920s, $4-6

Guests at the Desoto Hotel enjoying the swimming pool.

Circa 1920s, $4-6

Another view of the Hotel Desoto's swimming pool which was "filled with artesian water from our own well."

Circa 1920s, $4-6

The elegant Sapphire Room in the Hotel Desoto, "A Southern Paradise."

Cancelled 1949, $8-10

The Tavern at the Hotel Desoto.

Circa 1920s, $5-7

The Forsyth Apartment Hotel the location of "Savannah's finest apartments" situated near Forsyth Park.

Cancelled 1947, $6-8

HOTEL WHITNEY — SAVANNAH, GA.

The Savannah Hotel located on Bull Street, was designed W.L. Stoddart and opened in 1912.

Cancelled 1923, $6-8

Facing Johnson Square, the Hotel Whitney was "one of Savannah's best," since demolished.

Circa 1920s, $5-7

Savannah Hotel, Savannah, Ga.

The Hotel Savannah "the South's most beautiful fire-proof hotel."

Cancelled 1915, $6-8.

Hotel Savannah, Savannah, Ga.

Hotel Savannah, "Savannah's largest and finest hostelry."

Circa 1930s, $6-8

The Hotel Savannah as seen from Johnson Square and the Nathaniel Greene Monument.

Circa 1930s, $5-7

HOTEL SAVANNAH SAVANNAH GA.—108

Savannah was home to many beautiful luxury hotels like the Hotel Savannah located near Johnson Square.

Circa 1930s, $5-7

A view of the General Oglethorpe Hotel from the docks. The hotel offered fishing and hunting excursions in season.

Circa 1940s, $3-5

Located on Wilmington Island nine miles outside of Savannah, the General Oglethorpe Hotel was open to visitors all year round.

Circa 1940s, $5-7

The General Oglethorpe Hotel as seen from the Hotel's pool.

Circa 1940s, $3-5

Mrs Bannons daughter is Mrs Gambol of Ga

Savannah, Ga., Bannon Lodge, Thunderbolt. *Took dinner here yesterday*

The Bannon Lodge was opened in 1875 by Mrs. A.M. Bannon and was well known for its delicious homemade food.

Cancelled 1902, $4-6

Located on West 37th Street, the Awcomon-Inn was known as "the aristocrat of tourist homes."

Cancelled 1941, $7-9

The Hotel Pulaski, "Savannah's newest and oldest" hotel also located on Johnson Square.

Circa 1920s, $7-9

118

Another view of the "ultra-modern" Awcomon-Inn.

Circa 1940s, $7-9

The Poinsettia on West 37th Street Savannah.

Cancelled 1938, $4-6

Also located on West 37th Street, the Cozy Inn was situated "off from corner away from noise."

Circa 1940s, $7-9

The Pulaski Hotel, "Next door to theaters and shopping district. In close proximity to many points of historical interest."

Circa 1910s, $9-11

HOTEL DE SOTO, SAVANNAH, GA.

The Hotel Desoto was "Superbly located" on Bull Street and was originally open to visitors fall, winter, and spring.

Circa 1930s, $3-5

In addition to a marvelous swimming pool, the General Oglethorpe Hotel was also home to well-known golf club.

Circa 1940s, $3-5

Visitors stand on the dock and admire the General Oglethorpe Hotel, located "On the Enchanted Isle."

Circa 1900s, $6-8

Trees shade the side of the Hotel Desoto "the principal hotel of Savannah."

Circa 1910, $6-8

Islands and Beaches

Savannah is surrounded by beautiful countryside – the islands, beaches, and small suburban communities that make up the Low Country of Georgia and South Carolina.

Communities like the Isle of Hope were established in the 1800s as summer retreats for city residents, where they could escape the intense summer heat, as well as malaria outbreaks. Tybee Island has played an important role in Savannah's history. The first structure built on the island was the original Tybee Lighthouse, completed in 1736. The lighthouse has been rebuilt several times over the years and has served the city as a beacon to guide ships through the shallow waters at the mouth of the Savannah river and later as a museum and historic site.

Swarms of mosquitoes and other pests made life miserable for the island's early settlers. Around 1851, visitors were traveling to Tybee Island for "outings" but they rarely stayed for more than a few hours. In 1873 John Tebeau began planning to subdivide the island for further development. A hotel called the Ocean House was built in 1876 and in 1886, a railroad was built connecting Tybee Island with Savannah.

Only eighteen miles away, Tybee Island is a warm weather draw for resident and tourist alike in Savannah. An excursion to the beach was a must for any Savannah tourist. The beach itself was described as "Georgia's most popular playground" and it was a fairly accurate description. The climate in Savannah is subtropical which means that people can enjoy the beach for a good part of the year.

The road to Savannah Beach was as much an attraction as the beach itself. The route to the beach lays on the route to Tybee Island and features several interesting attractions including the famous Fort Pulaski, named for the famed Revolutionary War hero Count Casimir Pulaski, the first military assignment of then West Point graduate Robert E. Lee, and the first military engagement in which rifled cannons were used.

The walls of Fort Pulaski, the holes in the walls come from cannon balls fired by Union Troops who captured the fort in 1862.

Circa 1910s, $4-6

Sun bathers frolic on Savannah Beach, "Georgia's most popular playground."

Cancelled 1933, $6-8

HOTEL TYBEE, SAVANNAH BEACH, GEORGIA

The Hotel Tybee had "150 rooms of perfect comfort, delightfully cooled by ocean breezes."

Cancelled 1943, $3-5

23—Enjoying a Swim in the Atlantic Ocean
Savannah Beach, Georgia

Beach-goers swim in the Atlantic Ocean at Savannah Beach, now Tybee.

Circa 1940s, $3-5

HOTEL AT TYBEE, NEAR SAVANNAH, GA.

Tybee Island has been a popular Savannah tourist destination since 1851.

Cancelled 1908, $8-10

DE SOTO BEACH
HOTEL

De Soto Beach Hotel

SAVANNAH BEACH
GEORGIA

Like its counterpart in Savannah, the De Soto Beach Hotel was a popular destination for visitors.

Cancelled 1945, $6-8

De Soto Beach Hotel
SAVANNAH BEACH, GA.

Moonlight and High Tide, Wilmington Island, near Savannah, Ga.

The salt marshes on Wilmington Island at high tide. Wilmington Island is a home for permanent residents and a destination for tourists alike.

Circa 1940s, $2-3

An aerial view of the De Soto Beach Hotel located "On the Atlantic Ocean."

Circa 1940s, $4-6

The Isle of Hope was a popular summer retreat for wealthy Savannah residents. Some of the older houses on the island date back to the 1840s.

Cancelled 1914, $6-8

Isle of Hope, Near Savannah, Ga.

New Pavilion, Tybee Beach, Tybee Island, Savannah, Ga.—1

The first Tybee Lighthouse was built in 1736 by James Oglethorpe. The current lighthouse tower was built in 1867.

Circa 1940s, $3-5

The old pavilion on Tybee Beach. Tourists often came to Tybee Island on vacation but there were very few permanent residents before 1873.

Cancelled 1920, $6-8

Tides Hotel Apartments on Atlantic Coast
Savannah Beach, Georgia

For visitors who stayed more than a week or two some hotels like the Tides offered "completely furnished" two, three, and four room apartments.

Cancelled 1957, $6-8

Palm trees and oleander bushes line the road to Savannah Beach, "Where ocean breezes blow."

Circa 1930s, $2-3

PALM TREES AND OLEANDERS ALONG BEAUTIFUL DRIVE TO SAVANNAH BEACH, SAVANNAH, GA.

OA3943